Ghetto of the elect. A wall, a ditch.
Expect no mercy. In this most Christian
of worlds, the poet is a Jew.

Marina Tsvetayeva

ALSO BY IRVING LAYTON

Here and Now/1945
Now Is The Place/1948
The Black Huntsmen/1951
Cerberus (with Louis Dudek, Raymond Souster)/1952
Love The Conqueror Worm/1953
In The Midst Of My Fever/1954
The Long Pea-Shooter/1954
The Blue Propeller/1955
The Cold Green Element/1955
The Bull Calf and Other Poems/1956
Music On A Kazoo/1956
The Improved Binoculars/1956
A Laughter In The Mind/1958
A Red Carpet For The Sun/1959
The Swinging Flesh (Poems and Stories)/1961
Balls For A One-Armed Juggler/1963
The Laughing Rooster/1964
Collected Poems/1965
Periods Of The Moon/1967
The Shattered Piinths/1968
Selected Poems/1969
The Whole Bloody Bird/1969
Nail Polish/1971
The Collected Poems of Irving Layton/1971
Engagements: The Prose of Irving Layton/1972
Lovers and Lesser Men/1973
The Pole-Vaulter/1974
Seventy-Five Greek Poems/1974
The Unwavering Eye/1975
The Darkening Fire/1975
For My Brother Jesus/1976
The Poems of Irving Layton/1977
Taking Sides/1977
The Uncollected Poems of Irving Layton/1977
The Covenant/1977

EDITOR

Canadian Poems 1850-1952 (with Louis Dudek)/1952
Love Where The Nights Are Long/1962

The Tightrope Dancer

IRVING LAYTON

McCLELLAND AND STEWART

Copyright © 1978 by Irving Layton

ISBN: 0-7710-4871-8

CANADIAN CATALOGUING IN PUBLICATION DATA
Layton, Irving, 1912-
  The tightrope dancer

Poems.
ISBN 0-7710-4871-8 pa.

I. Title.

PS8523.A98T53   C811'.5'4   C78-001229-1
PR9199.3.L39T53

McClelland and Stewart Limited
The Canadian Publishers
25 Hollinger Road, Toronto

Printed and bound in Canada

For Gypsy Jo

CONTENTS

FOREWORD

When I was just starting my career as a poet, someone told me that there were only two subjects worth writing about, sexuality and death. I didn't understand then what he meant, but I do now. The poet, either through genes or genius, is poised on a rope stretched tautly between sex and death. The major poet dances on the tightrope; the minor poet walks warily across it. The non-poet or poetaster, rapidly becoming one of this country's major home-grown products, doesn't even make a try at either. The literary scholar and the critic remain, of course, solidly and securely on the ground, fussily adjusting their binoculars and peering intently through them, once they have found what they believe is the right focus for watching the performance on the tightrope.

Someone else said, "When writing a poem, get the first line, get the last line, and bring the two together as soon as you can." This excellent advice has made me want to avoid the rant and rubbish taken for poetry by those perennial *culturati* whom poets in every age must contend against: the faddish, the foolish, and the ig-norant. For me, poetry has meant packing maximum meaning and intensity into every line; if possible, into every word. A poem should resonate in the mind and heart long after it has been heard by the ear. Anything else, whatever my lapses in practice, I've always considered rhetoric or journalism; or short stories arranged vertically on the page, easy to read and even easier to forget. A poem, when you are done with it, must be able to get off the page, turn the doorhandle, and walk directly into the lives of people.

Poetry, whatever form it takes, is an arrangement of words whose vitality endures from generation to generation. Since this is an age of atrocity, when sadists and torturers proudly wear their decorations at public functions; when terrorists who gun down helpless women and children are hailed as heroes; and when thugs and despots are listened to politely as they expound their views on human rights, it is difficult for the true poet to restrain his pity and contempt for the human condition as it is revealed to him in the present century – difficult for him to write for human beings who accept the enslavement and murder of others without protest or execration.

Perhaps the poet's tightrope is not stretched between sexuality and death, but between love and loathing for the human race. Lacking the assurances of the theologian or the smugness of the logical positivist, the poet finds that this is not an easy age in which to live or create. He sees too far ahead to be complacent or comfortable. Unlike the economists and sociologists with their charts and graphs, he knows that the problem isn't inflation or bad housing, but man himself, and that a sharp drop in the price of oil or coffee beans, for all the excitement such a drop would occasion among editors, congressmen, and parliamentarians, would do nothing towards solving the central moral and psychological dilemmas of our time.

There's a huge possibility that the "ism" that will triumph over all the other competing "isms" in the near future will be cannibalism. Will the erudite cannibal want to read Shakespeare or Goethe? I wish I could shout a loud and confident "NO!" But human nature has revealed itself to be infinitely adaptable. Didn't men and women in the heart of Christianized Europe look on silently while six million people were murdered before their eyes, without any falling off in their attendance at operas, concerts, and poetry readings? How many people made any protest when those six million were being led off into the horrendous death camps or were being machine-gunned in the forests? Who? The pope? The German bishops? The Italian, Polish, Roumanian, French, Greek poets and short-story writers? Or maybe the protests came from distinguished film-makers, composers, and muralists?

At this moment, there are slave camps in the Soviet Union and its client states. The prisons in Poland, Roumania, East Germany, Bulgaria, Cuba, Iran, Africa, and South America are overcrowded with dissidents and critics of their infamous regimes. Do the daily beatings, mutilations, and torturings – of which the well-fed citizens in those countries are of course fully aware – in any way interfere with the production of encyclopedias, violin concertos, or novel methods of assaying literary worth? Is the applause for the gifted ballerina or actor any less noisy or enthusiastic? Are the newspaper columns less fulsome in their praise of art and more adamant in their condemnation of atrocity, and are they less eagerly read? Is there any limit to the amount of mendacity and corruption human beings can be conditioned to accept? Personally, I don't think so; their capacity, I long ago concluded, is limitless; their resignation appears so complete and despairing. Culture, never to be confused with Art, is the big lie of our epoch, the lie that makes it easier to swallow all the others.

Still, it's hard, if not impossible, for me to break a habit that it has taken almost half a century to form. Today, only words, artfully shaped out of passion and integrity, have any meaning or validity for me. All other verbiage I regard as excrement on floral bumpaper. I recall saying to a friend, "When my head is soaped by time, I hope I shall have enough craft and wisdom to compose a handful of lyrics that say with concision and intensity what living on this beautiful and dangerous planet has meant." I am immodest enough to believe that such lyrics will be found in the present volume by the alert and sensitive reader, and am sanguine enough to think that such a reader still exists. When women, homosexuals, proles, and blacks are at last free and equal, people will still continue to experience grief and rapture, want sex, grow old, and die. Enduring poetry keeps these constants in mind, whatever the earth-shaking changes in foreign policy and government.

Irving Layton
Toronto,
March 28, 1978

FOR 751-0329

Your eyes are dark and tragic as history
as you stare at the postcard village in the distance;
you are a distinguished graduate from Auschwitz
and mankind's incurable viciousness,
and your slender arm with its tattooed figures
boldly displays your credentials to the world

Each time, my dear, I see your naked loveliness
on this deserted beach my heart is torn apart
by love and loathing, gratitude and disgust,
by reverence and rage until my frantic mind
scurries like that insect between the hot stones
and I grow deaf to all but the waves' savage gulps

And though I know that all the innocent dead
find their resurrection in us and every loving pair;
imaging the dateless horror of the death camp,
the lexicon of human villainy made plain,
I curse without ceasing into the sweet empty air
and feel my loathing for mankind grow as vast as the sea

INTIMATIONS

Wordsworth glimpsed heaven when a boy;
William Blake, remembering childhood,
composed "Songs of Innocence"

When I was a child three events
showed me I dwelt among the damned:

A whorehouse raid
and the derisive gelasmus of the crowd
when the sheepish men came out
holding their felt hats in front of them

The whip's lash across my face
a laughing carter dealt me
as his wagon raced past the one
I was stealing my joyful ride on

And the young hooligans
shrieking we were Christ-killers
when they hurled the frosted horsebuns
into my mother's grocery store

THE TIGHTROPE DANCER

Awareness of death's pull
into nothingness
begets tyrant and sadist
but the prod, the harsh shove of love
makes the defiant artist
dance on his tightrope

DANKE SCHÖN
For Nicky Fisher

Lady, thank you for sitting
quietly where you are,
gazing away from your companion
at the tawny leopard-spotted hide
of the mountain
and the blue-green sea

For nearly an hour
I have stroked your hair, your neck
and lovely shoulders;
I have run my fingers over your full breasts
many, many times
and with your connivance
slid my hand
between your opening thighs

Your laughter and smiles
I banked in my frenzied senses
as the merited reward
for my adoration

Lady, thank you for sitting there
and letting me fill my eyes
with the beauty of you

You have given me more pleasure
than the white buildings on the shore
or the blue-green sea;
you have given me more joy
than most people have given me
in a lifetime

Sifnos,
June 23, 1977

PUPPET SHOW WITH DIALOGUE

I must immortalize your breasts.

They sag.

Excellent. You shall possess
the only sagging breasts
poetry ever made immortal.

When I look at them
my despairing thoughts fall down
farther than they.

Nonsense. You must think of them
as humble resigned saints
kneeling for absolution.

Your conceit uplifts
neither my breasts nor me.

Well, then, your nipples:
they're two unopened rosebuds
dropped in the snow
to baffle an Alpine climber.
He plucks them from the snow
and starts an avalanche.

Worse and worse.
What can you say about my cleavage?

From the magnificent tower of your neck
it is a golden runway
for a flight into dark ecstasy.

Give me your hand, poet,
and let me fill your goblet
with wine.

I drink to you, O lovely lady,
and to your breasts
for they are the drooping eyelids
of a sleeping world dreaming
of perfection.

(The puppets, Poet and Woman,
clink glasses and embrace)

FOR ARTEMIS

When my merry village Greek
naked and bronzed by the sun
   lies down beside me
all the sea's pulses throb
with my great excitement
and I imagine the shadows
the surrounding rocks throw
   on the deserted beach
silent goat-footed satyrs
about to drag her into caves
   no human foot may follow

She is so lovely and desirable
I am an immortal god
   and I know with certainty
death is unreal, mere shadow-face
of sexuality, a foolish illusion
like the days and years men have invented
out of pride or idleness
   My hands are all over her
and when she bends into my body
I sigh and can no longer hear
   the gentle suck-suck of the sea

FIGS

At this hour
the figs
look like the tight green testicles
of a youth

Next month
they'll hang loose and furrowed
like an old man's

MADMAN ON MITHYMNA BEACH

My love, I can take everything
the world throws at me
   except your silence.
When I do not hear from you
the sun's only a distant fireball
and the sea nothing but an old gossip
repeating *ad nauseam*
   her one good story
to the impassive beachstones at my feet.

I try to fill up the silence
with recollections of your smile
   and perfect mouth,
your humorous melancholy eyes;
and sometimes I play with it
as if it were an accordion,
stretching and closing it between my hands
   to squeeze from it dear sounds
or I put it to my lips like a flute.

Ah, like a madman wanting
to strike fire from air I want
   to make your silence speak;
no, sing, whistle, hum, call me endearments
and whisper hoarse words of love
so that I shiver with remembered ecstasy.
My head resting on a stone for pillow
   almost I catch your voice, love,
until comes again the ponderous sea.

HUMMINGBIRD

Flaunting
their pirate's flag of pubic hair
in cool pairs
the firm-titted girls
go past me

Or they sprawl on the sand
giving their marvels to the sun

My turned head
is a hummingbird
sipping the dark flower
between their thighs

Myconos,
June 14, 1977

THE PAPAL ELECTION

I'd like to present
the present hard-working pope
with a present:
an authentic cunt-hair
such as I just saw
curling from the crotch
of a girl's too-tight bikini

If my darling
allowed me
I'd pluck a handful
from her magnificent black bush
and send one to each of his cardinals

After the champagne and oysters
after the love-making
with my plucked darling
who'd give a good shit
about the Decline and Fall
of Christendom?

Not I. I'd rather imagine
the cardinals relaxing
from their solemn agitations
over inversion, adultery
and the sinfulness
of making love to oneself
with one of them amassing
the cunt-hairs in his white pudgy hand
and inviting them all to play
"Who'll pick the longest?"
it being understood that whoever does
becomes the next pope in Rome

THE EXPANDING UNIVERSE

God came
and there was the Milky Way;
he came again
and there was Sagittarius
with its 800,000 billion stars

Each time he comes
he shoots another galaxy
into the sky

THE GOAT

The French tourist
is exclaiming over the sensitive face
of the he-goat. *Ah, comme il est beau!*
She is petite and with such charm
in the mere shrug of her shoulders
I almost bend down to kiss them

She raises her voice
in another exclamation of praise,
scaring the goat from the wall;
he runs no more than five yards
when he keels over, his refined face
smashing into some brambles and small stones

Hobbled. Like some older poets I'd known
back home, their balls in a Christian vise.
The goat would have sailed into the blue
had he not been trussed foreleg to hindleg.
Perplexed and bleeding and sad
his abashed face makes me want to cry

THE VOYAGE

The ship's speeding to Piraeus.
The intrepid gulls follow us
And islands doze like enchanted
Sea-monsters to disappear

At last, whisked off by Circe.
I take my disjunctions with me;
Though strong, the sun cannot melt them.
An albatross lies on my neck

Which every day I feed on lies,
Self-betrayals, and weaknesses.
No, I'm a chained Prometheus
Stuffing the bird that eats my heart.

I'm confused, fouled-up, in great pain
And only of one thing certain:
No postman is scuffing the waves
To bring me a letter from you

THE ORACLE

The filthy parakeet
speaks only classical Greek
to the sun-tanned faces
bending down to his bars

I'm not well up
on ancient Greek literature
but they could be stray lines
from Sappho or Callimachus

Like a spasm in feathers
he swoops from bar to bar;
he eats his own feces
and looks at me sideways
to see if I can take it

My anxious query
about the probable destiny of our love
angers him no end
for he begins to squawk
furiously

Before releasing a rude whistle
which is the nearest thing
to a Bronx cheer
on this or some other Greek island
any un-American fowl can make, my dear

FASCINATION

There are chameleons, crab spiders
and certain kinds of women

When my angel's with me
she quotes Hegel and Santayana
and scowls darkly as if the Sphinx
had asked her a riddle

When she's with a playboy
from darkest Manhattan or Chicago
she laughs like an idiot
and tells everyone to piss off

If she's talking to an obvious con-man
I'm ready to lay odds
she'll pull enough tricks of her own
to leave him begging his subway fare

And there are the hunting spiders
more ferocious and cunning than tigers;
when they strike they never miss.
Their innocent malevolence fascinates me

NIGHT MUSIC

I'm in the darkening courtyard
surrounded by a jungle
of flowers ferns and leaves;
above the gloom and leaf-spaces
the stars appear and disappear
like spectral moths caught in a net.
Far below the sea is wearing away rock and stone;
the hilltop castle is crumbling under the moon.

The small stray kitten I plucked
this morning from the cobblestones
is asleep in the hollow
between my knees. She purrs gently,
indifferent to Beethoven's "Kreutzer Sonata"
or yawns to show me her pink mouth and lips.
Only an occasional puff stirs
fern and leaf and flower,
the shadows they make on the terraced floor.

The music ravishes my ears, stirs
my heart and brain till I become
the blackness and silence that enclose me.
A sudden wind separates the black leafage
above my head, letting me glimpse
the bacterial smear in the sky.
The courtyard is full of small noises
as if Beethoven's notes were scattered
and scampering joyously over petal and fern.

The kitten purrs. Leaves and shadows stir
languorously. In my eyes are uncontrollable tears
for the frustration and futility
in each man's lot, the inadequacies
and confusions which are the burden
and *leit-motif* of the whole symphony.
No man so deaf that he can't hear it.
For me, from this night on all's changed.
I have hatched an asp that delays its bite:
there remains only to be desperate and brave.

Molibos,
July 28, 1977

THE FINAL POEM

I must go on with my crazy drives to the end;
in time my compulsions will become clear if not
to me then to everyone else, to my wife, friends,
children and to all who thought me a simple madman
sometimes vicious, most of the time laughter-provoking
in my passion to make rustless steel out of mere air

It is too late to whisk them out of my greying hair;
besides, they're not like dandruff to make a semi-halo
around my shoulders. The brush doesn't exist
that will free me of them, clear my head
and make it light and apostolical like my mother
who kerosened the lice out of it when I was a child

I'm insane enough to love two women
both ravishing, both good in bed, both equally sure
I'm that rarest of geniuses, one who's well-hung
and without a trace of sadism in his make-up.
The trouble starts when they offer me
two opposing lifestyles, two opposite destinies

For the years still to fall from the calendar.
Take my word for it, the disjunction has given
my inflamed pebbles a turn for the worse.
O race of shallow materialists, shallower cynics,
the fruits of love no man however wise
can quite foresee; and I'm a compulsive Heracletean

Cruelly racked by ambivalences. I must have
two of everything: tape-recorders, billfolds, poetic visions.
I never leave a store with only one hat or scarf.
Such amassing must content the self and anti-self
or were I toplofty as William B. Yeats I'd say
the man and his mask or something equally flaunty

For pedants who earn their chops decoding
the graffiti one writes on the walls of God's lively
ciborium. Well, they'll come for me at the end
when I stiffen in my love's arms – eeny, meeny, miny, mo –
and should an imp of Lucifer hear me moan or pule
I'll do penance and write my final poem in Hell

BRIDEGROOM

Submissively the young camel
kneels before the altar
to receive his cumber

As he raises the load from the ground
his thin lips flutter
with pride and satisfaction

Superciliously
he trots down the church aisle,
his hooves making a soft sound

TELL IT TO PEGGY

We're in this
together, love,
like a head
in a bear-trap

My head
. your bear-trap

YOU COME TO ME

You come to me
with your hair dyed henna red,
capped teeth, expensive rings.

You enfold me in your braceleted arms,
seeking safety and completion
in my head against your breast;
my smile, my innocent blue eyes
give you hope
and I feel your hunger
to make me your catastrophe,
your best excuse for rage
against nature's tyranny
as your womb does a somersault
against your quivering lips.

How can I help you?
You need a reason for living.

I don't.

ODD COUPLE

To get her to understand him
he spoke with eloquence and wit
yet chose his metaphors carefully

Alas, she was deaf

He painted a huge beautiful canvas
Picasso and Chagall might have envied
and stood it in front of her

Alas, she was also blind

Using Braille
he constructed for her intellect
a philosophy as original as Plato's
more dynamic than Nietzsche's

She had no intellect. She was also dumb

So now every night they play
three games of gin-rummy
and just for the hell of it
she sometimes lets him win

THEATRE

Like an oriental despot
settling into his bath
the sun drops slowly
into the sea

Attending its declension
with melons and retsina
the couple cry their amazement
"It's sinking" "It's going down"
wife and spouse vying
for the more inventive comment

They think sea sky and sinking sun
are actors waiting for their applause
and I almost expect them to rise
and cheer wildly
when the sun at last disappears

Their hand-clapping so persistent and loud
the sun, blushing, bounces back
for a curtain-call

Molibos,
July 15, 1977

GOODNIGHT, SWEET LADY

Ah, the rapture
of all the desire accumulated
over souvlaki and retsina
discharging itself
in the first kiss

The delight of fusing
two souls
in the perfect surmise
of knowledge and passion

The ecstasy
of putting fumbling words aside
in mutual surrender,
our bodies undulating on the dark floor
like seafern

Before building
into disagreements building slowly
into brabble and discord
that moderate in the tedious hours
into petulance or apathy,
the final onslaught
of revulsion and hate

Goodnight, sweet lady; ah, goodnight
goodnight

TRAPPED FAUN

And this one thinks she's a free soul
because she lets her shapeless tits hang out
and shows the crack in her ass
when she dances around the room
for the Greek soldiers

It all comes from winning
a horserace when she was fourteen
and later getting her picture in the papers
leading a student demonstration
at Trinity

When she gives her loud crazy laugh
and rolls her green eyes, opening them wide,
I know she wants to be taken for a trapped faun;
instead I sweep up the bra for her
and she snarls at me as no faun would

Persuaded the whole world is looking on
and taking the noise of the pistons
for loud applause
one day she will throw herself
under the wheels of a moving locomotive

TO BLOW A MAN DOWN

Between her legs, in her perfumed hole
You'll find there my twisted heart and soul;
All for love, my friends, all for love
I stuffed them in with a single shove.

To leave them in her moist orifice
Nothing I deemed as sheltering as this.
It gave her steps a peculiar walk
But all whispered they improved her talk.

She's taken my heart and soul away,
Her discourse refined in every way;
She's gone, my transformed gypsy, she's gone
And there's no one to blow a man down.

MEDUSAS

Flourishing nature's oriflamme
her gonfalon of hurt
medusas drop from wavecrest and white foam

In cities they wear fawning smiles
speak only to deceive
and possess two eyes
out of which look cruelty and lust

Observe: among them only poets and saints
are kind, having been born cross-eyed

Listen to the feral cries
of the wild-eyed medusas:
I'm a Christian, I'm a Maoist,
fascist, Marxist, nationalist
I believe in progress and the rights of man

Foamblobs
time's ever-ready spike deflates
and smears like the brown scum
on the rocks below my feet

In Greece, jellyfish are called *medusas*.

SCHADENFREUDE

They gather around him like pigeons
waiting patiently
for the bad news to drop from his mouth

The commiseration in the glances
they give him
is an accurate index
of their happiness

They pass their compassionate smile
from one to another
like a thin religious wafer
that lights up each face

The first scoop is the best
and like no other

But the flutterings can go on for hours

PROVENDER

Unfailingly I feed my acquaintances
in the agora
tidbits of personal grief
invented or real

Then as the village and the sea
become silent and beautiful
I run to the butcher-shop
for slices of sheep's lung
to bring my kittens

I love to watch them cleaning
their frail whiskers
slowly and daintily on my doorsteps
and to overhear their delicious purrings

Molibos,
August 21, 1977

AT THE CHILL CENTRE

Between cliff and cliff
someone tightens the sky
like an Assyrian bow

I muse on drowned sailors
and violent undersea deaths;
on the viper's hood
emblazoned by the sun,
the Medusa
at the chill centre of the world

I would be the innocent waves
devouring one another with glee

Alas, I dwell among metaphysicians
and sadists;
in between shuffle
the hordes of unfeeling philistines

FOR ANOTHER WHO SQUEEZED BACK
For Rita

Because you squeezed back
I forgot everything life had shown me
of the hideousness of the middle-class

Especially of pastrami-devouring Jews
with marriageable over-ripe daughters
brunching Sundays at Yitz's or The Bagel

Would you believe it, I wholly forgot mediocrity
relentlessly transfigures them from birth
into gobs of sour offending flesh

Or how lies, my dear, the cynicism of the defeated
are their clipped and smooth coinage for buying
houses and footgear

Handbags lovers and graveplots.
I forgot Culture is the disinfectant they use
whenever they assemble in large numbers

i.e., in theatres and concert halls
and that even the dismayed gods are impotent
to make a silken verse from a sow's rear

How absurd that because you squeezed back
your perfume bottles mags etc. are in the hallway
waiting for you to pick them up at one-thirty

Toronto,
March 18, 1978

THE MALEDICTION

Little Jewish boy,
your face pale with terror and confusion,
let me utter the malediction
torn from your numbed lips
when the brutal German guard
pushed you into the gas chamber

"All who had a hand
in my death, I innocent and still a child,
who prepared for it in books and pamphlets
lectures seminars and talks
sermons and political speeches;
who scorned my people
and drew up the blueprints and timetables
for their execution
and gave the orders or carried them out
and all who looked on and approved
while they were driven like cattle
to this slaughterhouse
across the human wastes of Europe:

If you are yet alive
may you this instant be seized with convulsions
till your eyes are shaken from their sockets;
may your bodies begin to rot
and give off such vapours
that you almost suffocate from them
as one by one
your decomposed limbs drop off;
and let there be no salves or cures for you,
no analgesics or pain-killers

but may you live
one hundred and twenty years
and till the hour of your deaths
hear no other sounds
but your own groans

But if you are dead
having died peaceably
and been buried with grief and decorum
may the just earth expel your remains
from its disordered bowels
like vomit like black excrement
and may your progeny
die choking in it
as I died that horrible day
clasping my mother's convulsive hand''

DON'T BLAME THE APPLE

Original sin:
to look
and to be happy.

No human
will forgive you that.
Not ever.

Not even your mother.

TO THE VICTIMS OF THE HOLOCAUST

Your horrible deaths are forgotten;
no one speaks of them any more.

The novelty of tattooed forearms
wore off quickly; people now say
your deaths are pure invention, a spoof.

More corrosive of human pride
than Copernicus or Darwin, your martyrdoms
must lie entombed in silence.

The devil himself is absolved, polyhistors
naming him the only fascist in Europe
ignorant you were changed into soap and smoke.

That's how the wind blows. Tomorrow
some *goy* will observe you never existed
and the Holocaust your just deserts
for starting wars and revolutions.

I live among the blind, the deaf, and the dumb.
I live among amnesiacs.

My murdered kin
let me be your parched and swollen tongue
uttering the maledictions
bullets and gas silenced on your lips.

Fill, fill my ears with your direst curses.
I shall tongue them, unappeasable shades,
till the sun turns black in the sky.

HANGOVER

I can't help it
if I hear a German speak
especially if he's a Catholic
from Bavaria
or for that matter
a Lutheran from Saxony
I want to ask him
whether his father
had been a Storm Trooper
or perhaps one of the guards
in Buchenwald
and whether his dear mother
had gone to school with Ilsa Koch
and I shudder
so that people notice it
when he strokes an animal
donkey or kitten
or even sticks his face
into the innocent leaves
of a plumtree
but whether from grief or rage
or some other emotion
I cannot tell

THE LATEST WRINKLE

Last night at the Neptune
sipping my thick coffee and cognac
I heard the woman exclaim
and believe me everyone
there was such tenderness
and unmistakable depth of feeling
in her voice,
a real unaffected sincerity
her words burnt themselves into my mind:

"Some of my best friends, Mr. Cohen,
   are Jewish survivors from Majdanek
   and Auschwitz!"

RABBI SIMEON COMFORTS HIS FLOCK

My abused people
you go staggering under blow after blow:
Germany, Russia, Poland.
Always there's an Egypt to flee.

Children of sorrow and light,
you are God's seed
and His sower's hand
scatters you over the earth.

Others rest cosy and proud in empire
until your bleeding feet
traversing their soil in flight
erase them from His sight forever.

MISHNAH AND THE ETERNAL SHMUCK

After experiencing for nearly 2,000 years
the charity compassion and love
their Christian neighbours unfailingly showed them
in forced baptisms forced conversions
Inquisitions pogroms and holocausts;
after nearly 1,400 years of Moslem brutality
arrogance and perfidy
the rabbis twirling their matted forelocks
and their disciples piously twirling theirs
still earnestly dispute hour after hour
under what conditions
a ditch becomes a hole
and whose moral responsibility it is
should a stray cow
its dugs heavy with milk
fall into it
and break her neck

BEFORE THE MILLENNIUM COMES

My sons, when you hear men
speaking angrily on streetcorners
about justice and human rights
make certain the doors are locked
and your pistols loaded

THE HAPPENING

In the cauldron of the twentieth century
(thunder, lightning, and rain)
brewed with the root of hemlock
wool of bat, tongue of dog:
the fatal league of the *cognoscenti*
envious impotency has crazed
and the degraded hordes in the metropoles

Before that wave has broken
it will have overwhelmed
compassion and excellence
and driven poets and saints
to beg in the streets

Murderers will be crowned
in the public square
and criminals in high places
revered;
the equality of tyrant and slave
will be proclaimed by law

O fathers of scientific socialism
you were woefully wrong:
not the proletariat
but the afflicted intellectual
is the midwife of the old society
pregnant with the new

And our children, alas, are doomed
to live out their base lives
in the burgeoning shadow
his unroyal hump already
throws on the bouldered ground

ENGLAND 1977

One can say it's petrified putrefaction
for there's no stink of decomposition,
no visible rot exudes

And there's the illusion of activity
in the banks and palaces
manufacturing sweet-smelling unguents
for weary feet going graveward

Also, if you put your ear to the ground
you'll hear the escaping gases
whistling arias
from one of Wagner's better known operas

POETRY

Fresh horse-droppings
on the dusty road to Eftalou:
brown on light beige;
and a single butterfly
giving wings to a smashed bun

SUNSTROKE

That immense animal, the sea, cannot hear the loud growls it mutters at the shore that cages it in

The bright sun cannot see the silver coins it throws down recklessly on the animal's stretched-out body

The surrounding hills do not know they haven't moved from under their haze in over a million years

And the identities in various configurations and shades of brown do not know they are merely dots of perception lying on stones that look disturbingly inert and silent

Or that on the moment's impulse I invite them into the fellowship of suffering and ephemeral glory though the bleached stones remind me of the harrowing skulls in the first filmclips of Auschwitz

The crumbling Genoese castle that the centuries have nudged gently tilts towards the silenced discothèque

And alone on my prayer-mat of sand I will myself into wholeness, fusing volition appetite and consciousness into a single ecstatic pulse of being

Between the outstretched arms of my protecting cove the water ripples like an accordion bestowing the most enchanting music

And suddenly the hills begin to move and I feel I am becoming the ears with which the sea hears its muttered growls

And the eyes of the bright sun watching the silver coins it tosses so extravagantly glittering on the sea's body

Lesbos,
August 23, 1977

58

DIALECTICAL LEAP

Nah, Herr Marx,
expelling utopian lunacies
with your cigar smoke,
it ain't the proles
grown bourgeois and fat
eating capitalism
(except in Russia
where they eat shit)
that are changing the world

Everywhere on this planet
women blacks and gays are;
and I have a ridiculous picture
I can't shake from my head
of you sitting on your stool
and singing the old Wobbly refrain:
"The working class can kiss my ass"
as you watch history swerve past
your discomfitted bust

FLIES

1.
God's black angels
can't help alighting
on my arms and shoulders
and irritating the life
out of me
when I'm trying to take
an afternoon snooze

And I can't help
squashing the life
out of them
and smearing their pasty guts
on the walls

2.
On the flypaper
they look peaceful
as if they'd been
suddenly overwhelmed
by the sweetness of life,
not at all
like the grimacing corpses
in the *Catacombe dei Capuccini*
their number and death-like silence
remind me of

3.
The pale yellow strip
studded with their
black stiffened bodies
and swaying in the gentle
morning breeze
is not without a certain
kind of beauty,
like my mother's cursings
preserved in amber
or Baudelaire's
Flowers of Evil

THE DESCENT OF MAN

Whatever those amiable liars tell you
– anarchists theologians poets –
keep this well in mind, my sons:
men have been known to go
from ripping out a woman's breasts
or cracking a child's head
as if it were a hazelnut
to cracking a joke
(paranomasia intended)
to make all their banqueting friends
and relatives
double up with laughter
and commend their wit

Do you think a mere untrained gorilla
could ever do that?

MEMO TO SIR MORTIMER

When you come
for me
      or for any
of my friends
please spare us
the preliminaries

FOR OLD RABBI SCHACHTER

"You may laugh at men's follies,"
my venerable rabbi said,
turning to shake
a withering finger at me
"but never, my child, scornfully.
Men also are fallen angels, you know."

He's been dead past fifty years
that dear simple man
and not a trace of him remains
except those artless words lodged in my head
yet were I now to laugh out loud
it would be at his folly for speaking so.

GOD IS NOT DEAD

Observing how my kittens attack
the raw sheep's meat I bring them each morning
for breakfast
and afterwards listening to their ferocious purr
suddenly it hits me
I've overlooked a significant angle
in this bloody arrangement of one species
feeding on another:
the joy of the predator
as he mangles and devours his victim
with his teeth and claws

Even Jack the Ripper must have known happiness
when he slashed the throat of the London prostitute,
known it again and again;
and think of the great joy
victorious generals must know
as they focus their binoculars on the bodies
of the enemy dead
lying forever stilled in ditch and ravine

There is a God after all!

DR. SPOCK PLEASE ANSWER

Why, the young man asked me,
when I am stroking the kitten
affectionately
and am gladdened by her loud purr
under my caressive fingers
why do I have a sudden desire
to strangle her
and feel her warm body
go limp in my hand
I who am so gentle by nature
and can number among his forbears
rabbis and savants?

OPIUM

Only the rare few can live with doubt,
complexity that borders on chaos

They are the great-hearted sun-worshippers,
the true aristocrats, princes, and kings

A superstition is what the masses want,
the mental effluvium they call faith or belief

They yearn for an ignorance they can perish for
blithely or murder for with a good conscience

In our blood-stained era any broad strain
of Christianity or Marxianism will serve

Since for their immedicable ills and discontents
they need the solace of pie-in-the-sky, and always

They will demand relief from the horror
of seeing one's monstrous face in the mirror

And being that unique thing in the cosmos: a soul
forever tethered to an asshole

THE ACCIDENT

A sudden braking.

After the accident
one roadster was lying
on top of the other
though their occupants
were all dead.

In the harsh sunlight
the two cars looked
like two exhausted lovers.

STAR TREK

We look up at the sky; the soundless
empty dark surrounds us

Sagittarius has 800,000 billion stars

We are probably seeing some of them now

My oldest friend and I
are walking to the nearest *taverna*
for a cup of tea

That is the only thing that makes sense

Sifnos,
June 21, 1977

FLOWERS HE'LL NEVER SMELL
For John Angus McDougald

Sir Mortimer holding my hand,
I like to attend
the funerals of the very rich
and calculate the estate
of the deceased
(give or take ten million)
by the length of the *cortège*
and the eloquent struggle
one sees registered on the faces
of the heirs
between grief and greed:
on the countenance of the composed widow,
the pallid nuances
between vexation and decorum

Neither relative nor invited friend
I feel no sorrow
only a deep pity
for the putrefying slob
who'd made money and power his gods
when there were flowers to pick,
fresh cuntholes to probe;
only an indescribable ache
for the dull wasted years
and the long-drawn-out death he'd endured
like hero or martyr
till the time of his coronary
when they'd made it official
with flowers
and a luxurious casket
black and shiny as his Cadillac

SMOKE

Père Lachaise is so peaceful
so elegantly laid out
it affords its foreign visitors
the gloomy pleasure of a Racine tragedy

At the tiered ciborium
my girl observes some humorist
has had his initials engraved
on the letter-box urn: C.M.

Before the neighbouring one,
a dark oblong vacancy,
we embrace and kiss fervently
and then embrace and kiss again

Then lighting a cigarette
we each blow a puff of smoke
and watch it fill the narrow void
before it vanishes into the sunlight

THE PRIZE

For years he grew them lovingly
and because he was so devoted
to their glory, unfailingly
his entries won him top awards

One afternoon, his garden radiant
as the Garden of Eden,
reaching for his prize-winning rose
he felt the sharp sting of a thorn

The next day he was useless
from his collarbone down
and only with his wife holding him
will he ever walk again

AFTER A SLEEPLESS NIGHT

The fat fat Greek woman
with gold on her molars
holding her youngest daughter
by the hand

The child holding the small cat
in her arms

The cat holding the air
between its paws

I must strive to keep
that image in my head
on those black nights
when sleep is far from my eyes

Or that of her husband
bending over his hoe
as though in silent thanksgiving
for the early-morning sunshine

And the roadside flowers
gallantly displaying
the choking white dust
on their ripped petals

THE GREEK LIGHT

In some kinds of light
the human visage terrifies
with its script of egotism,
greed, smugness, imbecility,
the ignoble instincts surfacing
like mantling scum
around the eyes and mouth

I sometimes dream
of walking into a mountain village
and seeing around me
only headless bodies.
I put whatever face on them
that pleases me
and they all rise from their places
to bind my head with laurel

Whatever pious dunce believed
socialism, Christianity, Maoism
could reconstruct the human face,
make it pleasing and lovable,
never reckoned with this light

Ios,
June 28, 1977

GREEK DANCER

He dances around
the glass of water some tourist
has placed on the floor

He lurches, leaps, slaps buttocks and thighs,
his eyes closed in Dionysian ecstasy,
the trance of *kefi*

So he would have us believe

Yet all his motions betray him.
He may shut his eyes
but he no longer hears the god,
having lost the gift of self-absorption
he once brought to him on feet abandoned
wholly to the honeyed sweetness of life

The audience applauds
his mediocre performance

And he is sad, sad
there's no one in the *kafénion*
to be aware or care that the exalting fire
from which once leapt
the dancer's power and joy
has gone from him forever

WHEN DEATH COMES FOR YOU

When death
comes for you, my dear,
let him take you
like a candleflame
that is taken
from its wick
by a gentle stir
of wind
smelling of lilac

DEATH WASHES THE FACE OF THE WORLD

Death washes the face of the world
like the light-filled water
purling gently over the beachstones at my feet

Eternally and quietly
without cease it does its appointed work
cleansing the face of the world
so that the holy light of joy
may shine in pebbles, sunlit leaves,
flowers and vegetation
and beyond all these, beyond everything,
in the glad eyes of women and men

Molibos,
July 5, 1977

SIR MORTIMER

Sir Mortimer
put his hand
over the old woman's mouth
and stopped her dead
in the middle
of an imprecation

She fell back
into the armchair,
the unuttered moiety
rattling in her throat
while her bulging eyes
glared hideously
at the velvet glove
floating away into
the vanishing bright air

COMRADE

Whisper it to me
I swear I'll keep it a secret
from everyone
even from my wife and best friend

Honour bright and all that
I'll tell no one;
you can trust me
but tell me . . . tell me . . . tell me . . .

Whisper it to me softly
whisper it in your most solemn tones:
when will you come for Brezhnev
and the red Mafia in the Kremlin
and will it be by plague, assassination
or a burst blood vessel?

On second thought
don't tell me;
let it come, Death,
as a delightful surprise

Molibos,
July 6, 1977

THE PROFESSIONAL

To the thugs
in the KGB and the Mafia
Sir Mortimer is known
as the professional
who takes his time
never loses his cool
and uses his silencer only
at the end

Though their delaying tactics
are numerous
and occasionally successful
no one has eluded him
forever

WATCH OUT FOR HIS LEFT
For Leonid Brezhnev

I loved the way
you went up to Stalin
and felled him
with one blow

He didn't even once cry "Foul"
but just keeled over
with a single groan,
his famous moustache sweeping the floor

I know your fine record:
the despots you laid low,
the arrogant shitheads in high places:
in the end you always put them to sleep

I know when you finally connect
you'll lay him out clean and stiff;
once down the bum will stay down
and never rise to his feet again

YOU ALLOWED THE GENERALISSIMO
For F. Franco

You allowed him
to clean his feet and wings
after he'd flown off
from the spilled sugar

To explore
for a brief time
the opened marmalade jar

And settle peacefully
on the tablecloth
clean and bright
in the white sunshine

Then brought
your black-gloved hand
down

No cry. No blood. Nothing.

BEATITUDE

All I require
for my happiness
is a pen
and a sheet of paper
to put down
my unhappy reflections
on men
and the human condition

ARAB HARA-KIRI

Without
the nobility and hardihood
of the men from Nippon
but not lacking
in occasions
for mortification and shame
they do it
for one another
through assassination

ZORBA THE JEW

Though they know I write
dark poems
filled with misanthropy and foreboding
the villagers
seeing me dance on the cobblestoned streets
and hearing my constant laughter
in the *kafénions*
call me Zorba the Jew

I've even heard
some of the older Greeks say
I'm the only man with *kefi*
in the whole island of Lesbos

Molibos,
August 13, 1977

SIR

Some have wailed and trembled
at the sight of your empty sockets.
John Donne, an Englishman,
hoping you might be a Christian
addressed earnest sermons to you,
using certain elegancies of phrase
he thought would ravish you.
Count Tolstoi, a Russian giant,
was scared shitless.

I neither defy you
with books and bared chest
like a Parisian intellectual
nor do I show you a clenched fist
while waiting for the Metro
to take me to Utopia.
I am no religious old man
designing my stoop in heaven.

I have only praise for you and thanks
for paralyzing in mid-air
a hated schoolmaster's arm
and for squelching before my eyes
a thin-lipped rancorous brother-in-law
I loathed with all the fury
of a ten-year-old's innocence.
At your own discretion you rid me
of other nasty relations; and
of hypocrites, liars, bullies and fakes
that flourished like stinkweed
till you scythed them back into the earth.

Bravo, Death.
Yearly you thin the ranks
of life's enemies and detractors,
relentlessly carting away
the wolves and stoats in human dress;
and only through your good offices
is the world sifted and changed.
To come right down to it: Sir,
the greatest point in your favour
is that you permit us to hope.

CHECKMATE
For Vladimir Nabokov

"Come with me," Sir Mortimer said,
"but we'll have to leave behind
  your delicious Lolita."

"Gladly," replied the famed novelist,
  grimacing with pain,
"but first you must let me finish
  this crossword puzzle
  and get the last word in."

Slowly he printed it out
letter by letter: D-E-A-T-H

Sir Mortimer laughed indulgently
at the irrepressible old trickster,
sly and triumphant till the very end.

BRAVO, DEATH. I LOVE YOU

What men could not do, you did.
You let him have his vodka, his girls, his tantrums,
the limitless power to humiliate and injure;
you let him strut his vain hour
before the trick-mirror you keep for
two-legged rodents who kill for titles and glory; then,
your sickle around his neck like the arm of friend or lover,
you jerked him rudely towards you
while your hammer bonked him into eternal unconsciousness

What: you mean, Death, his pipe didn't charm you
or the pictures he had taken
with a child on his knee, the world-famous Uncle Joe smile
on his sly pockmarked face? No? You don't say!
But his moustache and beetling black eyebrows
surely they terrified you when you came for him?
No? Your patience with him finally at an end
you wanted him in his rightful place
beside the other mass killers, the bemedalled excrement
history squeezes out of the bowels of Time

Thank you, Death. You allow me the joy of imagining
the tyrant's worm-ridden body, Molotov's kisses
sliding off his ass
to make greasespots on the coffinwood
beside those of Gromyko and Kosygin;
of picturing to myself
the playful moles hanging from his whitened ribcage
and his skull, hairless and severed, shaken
by the rattling vans on their way to the Kremlin

And once again
as I walk the unpaved lanes of my childhood
I count the dead rats on the ground, hot and steaming
after a July downpour,
and note the limp feet raised as if to brush the bronze flies
from their crushed faces.
The stench of decay and corruption almost makes me retch
yet I stay, held by their grotesque inertness,
the stillness that surrounds them in the afternoon haze

They are vanished; gone, gone forever
and not a trace of them remains;
but the modern sick bullies you whisked off
– Mussolini, Franco, Hitler, Stalin –
time can never dispel or dissipate
the vomitous stink they left behind
that stays in the memory of men till history ends

Death, I love you
for butchering those butchers, those fiends in human form;
for carting away garbage, filth on feet,
in your spacious green bags and cleansing the air.
You've done this for mankind in every century
since its great adventure began
and you almost persuade me
you serve one greater than yourself.
Anyhow, Death, bravo and many thanks;
with Desire and Chance, always I shall reverence you
as one in my beloved trinity of gods

TWO WOMEN

For Bobby Maslen

Two women I once knew lie in these mounds of silence;
each in her own way was extraordinary.
One, rebel and feminist long before her time,
a Greek Georges Sand beautiful and defiant
whose distinction won her enemies everywhere,
the natural enemies of the aristocrat.
She took a lover in this Christian village,
loved and was loved while their loathing grew;
the men's out of baffled lust, the women's
because their mirrors showed them commonplace
beside the unfair radiance that was her portion.
Virtue is most often envy at another's grace
and never was so much virtue found in one place
as in this village where prodigal Stella
lived unabashed her turbulent life
till the grim dames changed her to a toothless crone
and sat her mumbling on her unwashed steps,
her legs thick as an elephant's, giving off smells.
Then, as if Jesus had come, envy changed into pity
and stone-hearted rancour into charity
and smiles wreathed all faces where once were frowns
till one morning when all the villagers were at church
the old decrepit iconoclast and rebel
whom so much Christian love had quite unhinged
poured kerosene over her tattered dress
and putting fire to it became the flaming torch
that always lights up for me her imagined face.
Her charred remains are under that stone
and here are my flowers for her unquiet grave.

The other was an American woman
deformed from birth who fled country and kin
fearing looks and derision for the small hump
she carried on her back like a snail's house.
It's difficult for the frail and weak to live
among the strong whom strength makes insensitive
to woes they may imagine but can never know.
Here in this village she lived among the humble
who pitied and loved her as an angel
who'd fallen from the sky and breached her spine
that mending had grown twisted as an olivetree.
And she gave back their love in full, detailing
their lacklustre village lives on canvases
glowing with her genius and affection
though her face never lost the stranger's smile,
the exile's grimace that still twists into my grief:
women washing their clothes, combing their hair,
the children sinister with birds and cats
and the men idling in the *kafénions*
or salting the fish in their wooden frames.
In her slow-paced crab-like walks she saw light
everywhere, filtering it through brush-hair
and acrylic: in the thin sentinel glasses filled
with ouzo, the furrowed faces of the village gossips
and the thick roadside dust on quincetree and vine;
always she proffered an ironic affection to the *pappas*,
their black beards parting the morning sunshine.
That's her grave, not five paces from Stella Ionnou's
and above the Greek inscription which translates
"Death exists only for those who are still alive"
her simple name salutes you. PEGGY SYLVIA

Molibos,
August 17, 1977

FOR MY BROTHER OSCAR

On October 25th Picasso's birthday
a leaf
in a rain of leaves
you curled up
on the steps of the Chase Manhattan
where you'd gone for the money
to fly you
into the radiant skies of Florida

You always were an ironist
my dear noble-hearted brother
gentle in everything
but your animus against life's
duplicity and pain
and your last pointed witticism
was undoubtedly your best

I laughed so hard
the tears are still rolling down
my cheeks

FOR MASHA COHEN

How could you curse the foul Cretin
who made this world,
your tongue black
and so swollen it filled the mouth?

We tried to discern
the old handsomeness
in the bloodshot beseeching eyes,
the silenced ash-grey lips.

Saliva and green pus for cosmetics,
on the white bed your wasted body
was held to a single function
– to chronicle the stabbing pain.

Wherever you are, Masha,
if it comforts you
we your friends cursed for you.

Toronto,
March 19, 1978

LATE INVITATION TO THE DANCE

Almost ten years have gone by since I first came to this village.

The same smells from the fields, the same breezes from the sea.

The same stars that have shot up and down that blue patch of sky above me.

The cypresses rising up in the dark like tall solitary madmen muttering to themselves about the night's intolerable sultriness.

The post office to my left, the garbage-collector's house to my right.

My feet make the same eerie crunch-sounds, I breathe a little heavier.

Under the white stars I carry in my headpiece the same unshakable faith in the holiness of reason, beauty, and love.

And in the same fragile headpiece the memory of affections, enmities, ambitions, the cruel words heard and said, the shameful deeds, and the glory of breasting the evil hours like a ship's prow.

My disenchantment with the human race that has hardened like cement or settled like a freshly dug grave over which hovers a single butterfly.

Revolutions, wars, assassinations, and the deaths of great and famous men – all the familiar troubles. And explorations into space to find God wandering among the galaxies and to bring him back to his creatures dying of loneliness and anomie.

Behind me, the same frenzied tourists in the *kafénions* wearing different clothes and faces, the same rueful Greek merchants rubbing their smiles together to strike fire from them, *kefi.*

Ahead of me, the same winding road on which you halt for a moment to gaze thoughtfully at the moon-polished sea and the small white-walled cemetery that in the distance looks like a gleaming skull someone has playfully rolled down into the valley.

Molibos,
August 21, 1977

THE MONSTER

The drains of Molibos
are an underground monster
you can hear stirring
in the hot months of July and August
far below the fairness of ripening fruit trees
and when leaf and fern are everywhere
an indomitable assertion of green

In our island enjoyments
of wine food sex and philosophical discussions
on the nature of God Man Society
when the sky is almost white with stars
and the imperial flowers
thrust their fragrance into the soft air
the foul breath of the monster
as he scrabbles
beneath gravel and cobblestone
or yawns noisily out of boredom
reminds us in the growing dark
of something we had not quite forgotten

Molibos,
August 4, 1977

FOR SASSU AND HIS HORSE

Your horses never ate hay

They leap out of the imagination
to cavort and neigh
on red undiscovered plateaus
and even when you limn men and women
there's something equine about them
– the greatest compliment you can give them

Blake had his tiger
Lawrence, his fox
Yeats, his deer with no horns
you, Sassu, have your horse
wild dynamic unreal
on which I ride with my corduroy heroes
Tom Mix and Buck Jones
into the fabulous world of my childhood
full of praise and wonder
making all men
trapped in the foul metropoles
by women or power
who see us thundering by
want to leap from the curb
on one of your mythical creatures
and direct him towards the red plateaus
and the waiting sun

YEATS IN ST. LUCIA

Thoughtless and primitive and selling
their woven blankets, these riant blacks
need your maunderings, O shade of Yeats,
like a hole in the head. Your fussy dialogues
smelling of lamp and planed for eternity
seem the self-indulgent fantasies here
of an unexercised man with a weight problem.
I see you climbing your famed tower
out of breath from years and tired lungs,
assaying the pros and cons
of Art and Life, Action and Thought,
and chipping neatly into place as you mount
the lines of your favourite puppets,
Soul and Body, Soldier and Poet,
and all the other brainy dialecticians
you shelter in your vellum pages.

As your portentous shade ascends
Thoor Ballylee, these excitable skinny Caribs
common and noisy in a marketplace reeking
of island spices and human sweat shout, sing
and show their strong white teeth;
insensible of your cultivated worries
or that you, Senator,
Poet, Playwright, Nobel laureate
and Lady Gregory's liveried patrician
after many subtle nictitations
at Art, the tinted mists of Byzantium
finally avouched your fealty to life.

To life as it's lived by men and women
coupling like toads in cemetery and ditch
or exercising their lithe beautiful bodies
on the soft white sands of their beaches:
beside royal palms and cow tamarinds
living always close to their instinctual wants,
the omniscience in their blood and loins
without your say-so or counsel, O blanched European
so laden with self-doubts and Irish mists.

THE PERFECT MOUTH

Never, I swear,
    in all my travels
did I see lips more perfectly shaped
so yielding, so soft,
the curve of them driving me
    out of my mind;
as did her chin's roundness

Hear me everyone:
    whole nights I could not sleep
for thinking of her perfect mouth
and in broad daylight
I'd stare at the subtle full lips
    like a blind man
who has just been granted sight

If I can have a last wish fulfilled
    I'll ask to see once more
the carmined orifice
that held me enslaved for so long.
I would forgive all, all,
    lies and mouth honour and deceit
on lips so perfect and beautiful

And watch once more the rose petals
    open on my manhood
to distil the familiar perfume,
making my frame twist with pleasure
as she draws the sperm into her faultless mouth,
    the final spasm
turning into my death quiver

SANDCRAB

On the white deserted beach
I've blocked the ingress
to his house;
he freezes with dismay
and I sense his panic
is no less
than that of the lyric poet
who watches his great gift
ebbing away
and with it his one excuse
to keep back self-contempt
and easeful death

THE JOURNEY

As if a mortician had laid him out
cross-armed cross-legged
the enormous toad looks pleased with himself,
the top of his battered head
baylaurelled with clots of brain and blood.

Having popped out from their skull
for a better look
the surprised eyes stare at it fixedly
from the wheelmark's hollows.

In the adjoining field
Elizabeth Taylor squats open-legged;
pees and chews her cud at the same time.

And tall against the pale sky
royal palms stand erect like Catherine's guardsmen;
how the fat queen loved to finger their testicles
when pondering weighty matters of state!

On the long white beach
I watch a sandcrab drag
my lit cigarette into his hole:
poet ransoming himself from guilt
through word-idolatry, himself the burnt offering.

Only at the town cemetery,
its many blistered arms outstretched
to embrace me,
do I deposit my burden of scorn and hate
in the first open grave I see:
one awaiting the charred remains
of a five-year-old child.

BLACKBIRD

He struts as if he owns the place
and his screech
at once querulous and triumphant
grinds scissors and knives
before he lets them fall
into the leaf-covered stillness

A lordly gentleman
in his suit of black satin
he's immensely pleased with himself
as he lifts
his reflection out of the pool
sips wide-eyed
or swallows the pink worm
he's plucked from the ground

He flits from chair to chair
a member of the leisure class
challenging my right to be here

I call him sleek arrogant bastard
I call him bourgeois
I call him merciless exploiter and parasite

His reply to all the Marxists
of the world
is a mocking whistle

St. Lucia,
December 21, 1977

TROPICAL FLOWERS

Beyond the window
pussytail and neighbouring cereus
O lovely Cinderella among flowers!
And the heart-shaped anthurium, deep red.

Sweet-scented frangipani, Turk's fez
Napoleon's button, blue petrea, golden trumpet
the spectacular poinsettia
flaming in the distance, tiger's claw
and the passion flower
haloed stand-in for my brother Jesus.

Bloom, flowers, and blaze
with bright persistence. Tendril by tendril
ignite the encircling air
and by your rooted sprightliness disgrace
the shivering decadents
too frail for the squalls and windstorms
of this world, the quaggy
sentimentalists with planned utopias
in their sick livers.

St. Lucia,
December 18, 1977

MOCKINGBIRD

Sea-sired the white rainless clouds
build random patterns, no vaporous Toynbee
marking their imperial shove
no corpulent Gibbon their rise and decline

Above the profusion of traveller's palms
and flowering trees that blaze like sunsets
the clouds melt into one another's arms
in a never-ending orgy of love

Lacking the delicate joy of hummingbirds
priests and sages seem lustreless beside
the smiling blossoms canopying
the fierce encounters of birds and insects

Platonist among trees, a solitary cow tamarind
affirms order and geometry
which the mockingbird from its very boughs
laughs at, laughing at life's eternal comedy

SUNFLIGHT

Brandy and milk. A young and fervent woman
who loves me. On my right, the sun
on loan for eleven halcyon days,
now lighting me on to St. Lucia.
Listen, down there: I live my fairytale
while my hair whitens to the movement of planets,
the groans of men and helpless beasts.
I have seen much, suffered much:
been in this beautiful and dangerous world
manloaf in the oven of some evil witch.
Now self-exiled from the great contempt
I climb toward those lustrous heights
whose guards are wisdom and joy.
My pride is the faint thumbmark humility
leaves on an aging defenceless ego
when I speak the resonant human lines
no prompter has ever scored, bending
over his long bank of ragged cloud.
Act 5, Scene 3. No corpses littering the stage.
No maniacal voices or screech of owls.
Scars, yes; wounds and woes. And remorse
that is vanity's sullen twin. Yes.
But now I adjust seatbelt and seat
and as the plane begins its swift descent
into the lush civilized jungle
I know again such ferverous delight,
such happiness without misgiving or guilt
as once in my fabulous boyhood long ago.

St. Lucia,
December 16, 1977

EDEN

We are back in the Garden of Eden
and the apple is still on the tree
or held in your delicate fingers
yet unbitten by you and me

And God is a voice in a bush
who wants our ignorant praise
and your graces are so varied, my love,
I bless my dower of days

Your kiss makes me tall as a palm;
I wave my fronds at the sun
till the flights of insects and birds
amaze me and stun

Our selves like the apple are whole
and nature and we are one
and there's no breach betwixt body and soul
under the coursing sun

HARRIETIA

Outside my room
oleanders and orange trumpet vines,
a profusion of tropical blossoms
blazing away.

Inside, my lovely Harriet:
a walking talking plant
that kisses and smiles
and whose tendrils embrace me
with a passion and fragrance
no flowering tree
may ever surpass or equal.

THE FINAL MEMO

Sir Mortimer
why did you do it?
Both terror and beauty
lie buried in a mass grave.

After Auschwitz and Hiroshima
who believes in funerals any more,
in the dignity
of dying for Cause or Faith?

You were the singular rod
by which we measured our lives,
its meaning and worth;
in your shadow we threw off radiance.

You were the supreme Antagonist,
majestic and severe;
almost we overcame you
with tragedies and religious myths.

By your excesses
you make a mockery of everything;
show us our lives are merely
a rumble of panic and grotesqueness.

GRAND FINALE

I've seen the grey-haired lyrists come down from the hills;
they think because they howl with eloquence and conviction
the townspeople will forgive their disgraceful sores
and not care much how scandalous and odd they look;
how vain their contrite blurtings over booze and women
or the senescent itch for the one true faith.

Not for me sorrowful and inglorious old age
not for me resignation and breastbeating
or reverbing of guilts till one's limbs begin to tremble
and a man's brought to his knees whimpering and ashamed;
not for me if there's a flicker of life still left
and I can laugh at the gods and curse and shake my fist.

Rather than howl and yowl like an ailing cat
on wet or freezing nights or mumble thin pieties
over a crucifix like some poor forsaken codger
in a rented room, I'll let the darkness come only when I
an angry and unforgiving old man yank the cloth of heaven
and the moon and all the stars come crashing down.

RETURN TO EDEN

You were sent to me
so that I could make my declaration of love
beside a Royal Palm
and kiss your small ears
under the Chorisia's white floss.

But everything that happened to me
before this
– what was all that about?

St. Lucia,
December 16, 1977

ACKNOWLEDGEMENTS

For permission to reprint I owe sincere thanks to the editors of the following publications, in which several of the poems in this volume first appeared.

CVII
Waves
The Canadian Forum
intrinsic
Toronto Life
Shark Tank
Origin
Tributaries
Canadian Literature

I also wish to express my very warm thanks to the Canada Council for a Senior Arts Grant that enabled me to visit different parts of the world to look over a new stock of metaphors, images, and symbols, and to test a wide variety of brandies, cognacs, cigars, and other delectable things I have found helpful to keep me a happy, born-again heathen and creative writer.